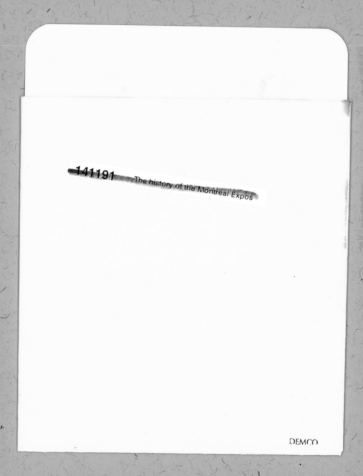

141191   The history of the Montreal Expos

DEMCO

PEDRO MARTINEZ

GARY CARTER

MAURY WILLS

RUSTY STAUB

MOISES ALOU

STEVE ROGERS

LARRY PARRISH

TIM RAINES

KEN SINGLETON

JEFF REARDON

ANDRE DAWSON

VLADIMIR GUERRERO

THE HISTORY OF THE

MONTREAL EXPOS

MICHAEL E. GOODMAN

CREATIVE C EDUCATION

Published by Creative Education, 123 South Broad Street, Mankato, MN 56001

Creative Education is an imprint of The Creative Company.

Designed by Rita Marshall.

Photographs by AllSport (Brian Bahr, Al Bello, Jonathan Daniel, Jamie Squire), Icon Sports Media

(Robert Beck, Chuck Solomon), National Baseball Library, Anthony Neste, Sports Gallery

(Al Messerschmidt), SportsChrome (Jeff Carlick, Scott Cunningham, Bryan Yablonsky, Michael Zito)

Library of Congress Cataloging-in-Publication Data

Goodman, Michael E. The history of the Montreal Expos / by Michael Goodman.

p. cm. — (Baseball)   ISBN 1-58341-215-8

Summary: Highlights the key personalities and memorable games in the history of the

team that has played in Montreal since 1969.

1. Montreal Expos (Baseball team)—History—

Juvenile literature. [1. Montreal Expos (Baseball team)—History.

2. Baseball—History.] I. Title. II. Baseball (Mankato, Minn.).

GV875.M6 G66 2002   796.357'64'0971428—dc21   2001047878

9 8 7 6 5 4 3 2

IN 1535,

FRENCH EXPLORER JACQUES CARTIER SAILED DOWN THE

St. Lawrence river in Canada and discovered an island dominated by a

large green hill and named it Montreal ("Mount Royal" in English).

More than 100 years later, French missionaries settled on the island

and the area around it, intent on bringing Christianity to nearby

Native Americans. By the late 1600s, Montreal had become a key

city in New France. Even though it passed into British hands in

1760, it retained much of its French heritage.

In 1967, Montreal, by then one of the most cosmopolitan cities

in North America, hosted a giant world's fair known as the Exposition,

or Expo for short. The event attracted wide attention, including that

of officials of major league baseball, who wondered if a baseball

GENE MAUCH

franchise could thrive in hockey-crazy Montreal. The executives decided to take a chance, and three years later, the Montreal Expos were added to the National League (NL).

{A COLORFUL START} Although the expansion Expos did not start off very successfully on the field, they were an immediate hit with fans, attracting more than 1.2 million spectators in their first season. The

The Expos took their lumps during the **1969** season, losing 20 straight games at one point.

team quickly became known as "Nos Amours" in Montreal, which is French for "our beloveds."

The team's first manager was veteran skipper Gene Mauch, known as the "Little General." He was a disciplined man who drove his players hard during spring training. "At the end of each day, I felt like an old sock in a washing machine," grumbled one Expos outfielder, recalling that first spring training.

The Little General's army included veterans such as infielder

ORLANDO CABRERA

Rusty Staub provided much of the of-fense during Montreal's first three seasons.

RUSTY STAUB

Maury Wills, a former NL Most Valuable Player (MVP) with the

Los Angeles Dodgers, and pitcher Jim "Mudcat" Grant. He also

commanded such youngsters as pitcher Bill Stoneman,

third baseman Jose "Coco" Laboy, and second baseman

Gary Sutherland.

The team's owners wanted the Expos to be

colorful to help arouse fan interest. Breaking from the

tradition of drab and simple major-league uniforms, Montreal's

players were dressed in bright red, white, and blue caps with a

fancy, multicolored "M" sewn on the front of each uniform. Then

the owners made a trade with the Houston Astros for colorful right

fielder Rusty Staub. His fiery red hair quickly earned him the

nickname "Le Grand Orange" from the French-speaking fans, and

his outgoing nature made him an instant favorite in Montreal.

Le Grand Orange and the Expos started off their first season

Pitcher Carl Morton did his best to lift the Expos in **1970**, striking out 10 batters one game.

CARL MORTON

The Expos have been playing "the American game" in Canada for nearly 35 years.

MICHAEL BARRETT

dramatically. Facing the Mets in New York on April 8, 1969, Staub belted a home run to highlight a wild 11–10 opening-day win.

The club won its home opener in rickety Jarry Park a week later in a game that was almost postponed because of snow on the ground. Three nights later, Bill Stoneman found a great way to warm up the Montreal fans when he tossed a no-hitter against the

Philadelphia Phillies.

There were few other highlights during that first campaign, as the Expos ended with a 52–110 record. But Montreal's fans were loud and enthusiastic, and it was clear that baseball had found a home on the north side of the U.S.-Canada border.

{GROWING WITH "THE KID"} The following season, Mauch promised more victories, announcing that the Expos would "win 70 in '70." They did better than that. Thanks to Staub's timely

KEN SINGLETON

hitting and 18 wins by pitching sensation Carl Morton—the NL's

Rookie of the Year that season—the Expos finished with 73 wins.

The Expos continued to improve in the early 1970s, but

Mauch knew that some changes were still needed to build a

contender. First, he made a strategic trade, sending Staub to the

Mets for three solid everyday players: outfielder Ken Singleton, shortstop Tim Foli, and first baseman Mike Jorgensen. Then, Mauch

made Mike Marshall his closer and promoted rookie pitcher

Steve Rogers to the majors. The new players helped

the Expos move up in the NL Eastern Division. In

1973, Montreal was in the pennant race until the last

weekend of the season, finishing a close second behind

the Mets. "Wait until next year," promised Mauch.

"These guys are just getting started."

Mauch had good reason for optimism. He knew that some

fine players were developing in the Expos' minor-league system.

In 1974, a young outfielder and part-time catcher from California

named Gary Carter and a fine third-base prospect named

Larry Parrish made their way up north. Three talented outfield

prospects—Andre Dawson, Warren Cromartie, and Ellis Valentine—

were also almost ready for the majors. It would take several years

Infielder Ron Hunt scored five times in a single game in **1974**, setting a new team record.

UGUETH URBINA

for the Expos to get all of these youngsters in place in Montreal, but

the wait would be worth it.

Montreal fans didn't have to wait long for Carter to become

a star, however. Nicknamed "the Kid" because of his youthful

appearance and enthusiasm, Carter had grown-up talent. In 1975, he

was named to the NL All-Star team as an outfielder. (Before

his career was over, Carter would make nine more All-Star appearances as a catcher.) Carter backed up his talent with a strong will to succeed. "If you put your mind to it, you can achieve what you want," he said. "Ambition has always been a great motivating force in my life."

Carter's career took a major turn in 1977 when he was named the Expos' full-time catcher by new manager Dick Williams. Carter developed into a steady leader on the field and an outstanding hitter, and the move also freed up a spot in the Expos' lineup for rookie outfielder Andre Dawson. Dawson soared into Montreal in 1977 and finished his first big-league season with 19 homers, 21 stolen bases, and the NL Rookie of the Year award. He also patrolled center field in Olympic Stadium (the Expos' new home) like a giant bird of prey, earning the nickname "the Hawk."

Gary Carter's great defense earned him the Gold Glove award every year from **1980** to **1982**.

GARY CARTER

Today's Expos hope to find success like that of the franchise in the early **1980s**.

With the Kid and the Hawk leading the

way, the Expos began a steady climb up the NL East ladder,

Tim Raines was a base-stealing terror from **1981** to **1984**, swiping at least 71 each season.

reaching second place in 1979. "Vive les Expos" ("Long

live the Expos"), Montreal fans began chanting as they

prepared for the 1980 season and what they hoped

would be a championship year at last.

Montreal got off to a fast start in 1980, with Carter

and Dawson knocking in run after run and pitchers Steve Rogers

and Scott Sanderson dominating opposing batters. The Expos went

into the final weekend of the season tied with the Philadelphia

Phillies for the division lead. The two teams faced off in Montreal in

a three-game series, and the Phillies won twice, ending Montreal's

hopes for a championship.

In 1981, the Expos felt they had found their final missing

ingredient in rookie outfielder Tim Raines. Called "Rock" because

TIM RAINES

of his stocky build and exceptional strength, Raines quickly

established himself as an excellent leadoff hitter and base-stealer.

Whether he was at the plate or running the base paths, Raines

drove opponents crazy.

With Raines's speed, Carter and Dawson's power, and outfielder

Warren Cromartie's solid hitting, the Expos were in the hunt for their first division title. The 1981 season was an unusual one.

Because of a players' strike in midseason, the year was divided into

two halves. The Phillies were the first-half leaders in

the NL East, while the Expos posted the division's best

record in the second half. Montreal then defeated

Philadelphia in a special division playoff series to earn

a spot in the NL Championship Series against the

22   Los Angeles Dodgers.

That best-of-five series came down to game five, which took

place in Montreal on Monday, October 19. The game was tied 1–1 in

the ninth inning when Steve Rogers came on in relief. He retired

the first two Dodgers batters but then surrendered a game-winning

home run to outfielder Rick Monday that shattered the Expos'

dream of a berth in the World Series. "It was a hanging slider,"

Rogers noted sadly after the game. "I wanted it to break down and

WARREN CROMARTIE

Andre "the Hawk" Dawson added both speed and power to Montreal's lineup.

ANDRE DAWSON

away, but it stayed up." For many years, Montreal residents also spoke sadly when they recalled "Blue Monday."

{THE DISAPPOINTING '80S} Expos fans were certain that the 1980s would be their club's decade of greatness. "We're the team of the '80s," one Montreal sportswriter declared. "With Carter, Dawson, Raines, and Rogers, what can go wrong?"

Standout reliever Jeff Reardon was sensational in **1985**, rolling to a league-leading 41 saves.

Unfortunately, the answer was "many things"—injuries, bad trades, and lineup experiments that backfired. Although some fine players, including first baseman Al Oliver and ace reliever Jeff Reardon, made their mark north of the border during the early 1980s, the Expos were never able to mount another serious championship run.

Beginning in 1985, Expos management began revamping the team's lineup in search of a winning combination. Carter was traded

JEFF REARDON

to the New York Mets for shortstop Hubie Brooks and several other players. Other new arrivals included first baseman Andres Galarraga, second baseman Vance Law, and pitcher Dennis

Martinez. This new crew helped Montreal go 91–71 in 1987, but disappointing finishes in both 1988 and 1989 completed a sad decade for Expos fans.

A new era

began in Montreal in 1992 when Felipe Alou—a longtime

outfielder and coach with the Expos—was named the

team's manager. Known for his patience and determi-

nation, Alou was an ideal choice to lead the young,

struggling Expos.

Alou guided the Expos to second-place finishes

in the NL East in both 1992 and 1993. The following year—with

outfielders Marquis Grissom and Moises Alou (Felipe's son) leading

the offense and pitchers Pedro Martinez and John Wetteland

starring on the mound—the Expos raced out to the best record in

baseball. Then, in early August, major-league players went on strike,

and the season simply ended. "A lot of things about the strike hurt,"

said Expos outfielder Larry Walker. "But having that great season

wasted is something I don't think I'll ever get over."

Marquis Grissom reminded fans of Tim Raines, stealing 154 total bases in **1991** and **1992**.

27

MARQUIS GRISSOM

Over the next few seasons, several key players left Montreal, mostly because the team could not afford to keep them. One

player that Expos fans hoped would stay was Pedro Martinez. The hard-throwing native of the Dominican Republic had developed into arguably the best pitcher in baseball. In 1997, he won 17 games with a stunning ERA of 1.90, recorded 305 strikeouts,

and was the runaway winner of the NL Cy Young Award. Then, the next season, Pedro too was gone, signing a free agent contract with the Boston Red Sox.

{THE GREAT GUERRERO} The 1998 season marked the beginning of a youth movement in Montreal. Two new stars emerged: right fielder Vladimir Guerrero and reliever Ugueth Urbina. At age 23, Urbina was the youngest closer in the majors. The flamethrower notched more than 100 total saves in his first

PEDRO MARTINEZ

three seasons with the Expos and was named NL "Fireman of the Year" by *The Sporting News* in 1999.

Meanwhile, Guerrero—with his rocket throwing arm and explosive bat—quickly established himself as the best young outfielder in baseball. Only 22 years old in 1998, Guerrero made headlines when he finished among the NL leaders in 10 different

Second baseman Mike Lansing hit two homers during a 13-run inning in one **1997** game.

offensive categories. He followed that up with back-to-back 40-plus home run seasons in 1999 and 2000. Pitchers weren't the only ones who feared Guerrero. Baserunners also quickly became wary of trying to advance on balls hit to right field. "[Guerrero] has all the tools to be outstanding, especially that arm," said Expos general manager Jim Beattie. "That's what people 'ooh' and 'aah' about."

While Guerrero and other rising stars—such as second baseman Jose Vidro, shortstop Orlando Cabrera, catcher Michael

MIKE LANSING

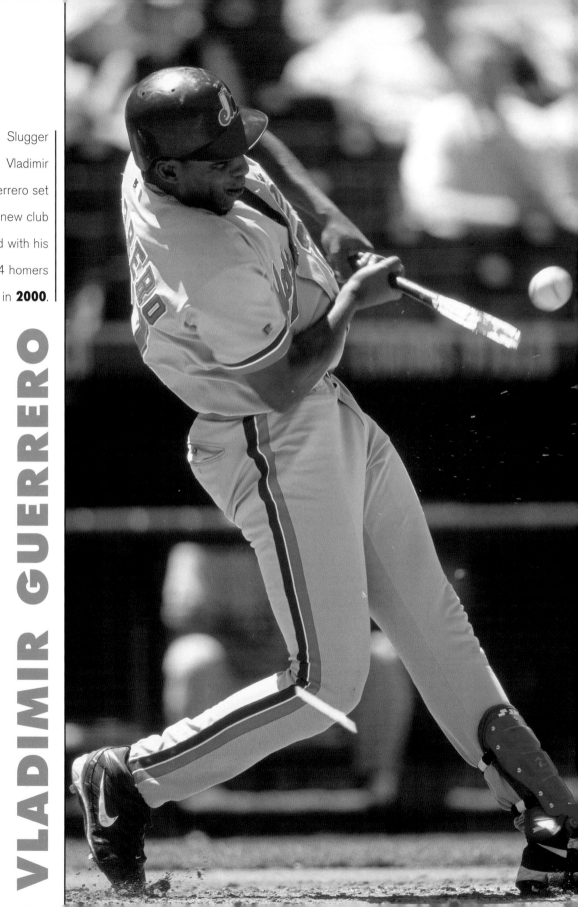

Slugger Vladimir Guerrero set a new club record with his 44 homers in **2000**.

VLADIMIR GUERRERO

Equally skilled in the field and at the plate, infielder Jose Vidro could do it all.

JOSE VIDRO

Barrett, and outfielder Peter Bergeron—improved in 2001, the team

continued struggling to win games and draw fans, leading to still

more changes. Urbina was traded to the Boston Red

Sox for prospects, and Felipe Alou was replaced as

manager early in the season by Jeff Torborg. Montreal

fans hoped that Torborg would have better success in

bringing the franchise back to life.

For more than 35 years, the Montreal Expos have brought

color and excitement to baseball fans in two countries and have

roused cheers from fans speaking in two languages. As the team

continues to seek its first World Series appearance, it also hopes to

once again have fans north of the border shouting, "Vive les Expos!"

CARL PAVANO